The RHYME and RHYTHM of CHILDHOOD

To Grace McCormick

May you cherish your memories!

Joyce Story
October 8, 2013

JOYCE STORY

Printed in the USA

ISBN: 978-1484051214

Website: www.JoyceStoryteller.com

Publishing Services: DMBookPro.com

DEDICATION

For my grandparents

George and Ethel O'Hara

Whose home in the small town of Hawthorne, Florida,

Was always open to family and friends

CONTENTS

INTRODUCTION

One of the highlights of family gatherings is the sharing of childhood memories. So it was with the author's kith and kin, and it was often her good fortune, as she grew up in northern Florida, to hear her relatives and friends recount tales of their early years. The stories in this collection were inspired by such memories and the events that formed them.

The author holds a doctorate in the field of literature and is a storyteller of many years' standing. Her time-tested stories are imaginative and engaging and offer something for everyone. No matter what their age, readers can take pleasure in the stories' playful qualities, which are enhanced by the creative use of rhyme and rhythm. The stories speak to young and old alike because they encompass both the viewpoint of the child and the understanding of the adult. Just as importantly, the themes--such as mischief and innocence, predicament and ingenuity, fear and daring—have meaning for us all.

TWO GOOD SHOES

I heard my mother shout
"David Lee!"
And I shrank inside myself.
My mother's voice,
Along with choice
Of name for me,
Spelled out
That I'd been bad
And she was mad.
I felt so small,
Not like a David Lee at all
But like a frightened baby.
I wanted Mom to hold me close
And call me little Davey.
But this is what she said,
"Come here, young man!"
I followed her command
With heavy heart and hanging head.

"And what is this?" she asked.
I wanted to explain
That I hadn't meant
To smear the honey on the floor
And on the kitchen door—
It was an accident!

"David Lee,
Knock off those sighs
And look, please, in my eyes.
You keep on staring at your feet!
It makes me think that you refuse
To talk to me
And choose,
Instead,
Your shoes."

And then I heard these words:
*"Of course!
No wonder!"*

Who said them? I didn't know the source,
But the softness of the tone
Was quite unlike the thunder
Of the anger Mom had shown.

Mom sent me to my room.
I turned on every light
And chased the gloom
Of night
Into a corner.
I heard that same familiar tone:
 *"Much better.
It's brighter now, and warmer."*
I slowly peered around,
But I saw no one there.
I glimpsed up
And glanced down,
Then quit looking for clues,
For what I had heard
Plainly came from my shoes!

Some shoes only walk,
But my shoes walked
And talked,
And what fantastic friends we soon became!
That night I showed them everything:
My favorite checkers game,
My purple plastic ring,
My lordly rubber lizards,
And my shiny silver scissors.
They loved my books and wooden case,
And how they oohed and aahed
When they gazed upon my squad
Of cars and trucks,
And ships from outer space!

"And now," at last they said,
"You'd best prepare for bed,
So get undressed and brush your teeth,
And give your mom and dad a hug."

I did as they advised,
And, wow, were Dad and Mom surprised
That I had brushed my teeth
All on my own.

Mom tucked me in and kissed me,
Then turned the light
Down low. "Sleep tight,
My little doodlebug!"

I murmured in content reply.
My shoes made not a sound,
And this is why...
They talked to no one else, just me,
And only
Then at certain times,
When I was lonely
Or was sad
Or scared.

Since Billy lived right down the street,
We always went to school together.
I really can't say whether
Billy
Ever knew the truth
About the bougainvillea.
It stood midway along the route
Between our houses and our school.
It towered over us and
Flowered in cerise
And attracted, like a magnet,
Swarms of bumble bees.
We had to pass the bougainvillea—
There was no other way—
And I would always guarantee
That Billy
Stood
Between that bush and me.

My two good shoes and I
Had been talking on the sly
About a month or so
When Billy pulled a low
Trick.
He got sick.
And that left me to go to school
All...
By...
Myself...

I swallowed hard
And set out on my way.
The bush loomed up ahead
Like a dark green dragon dressed in red
And I could hear—
Loud and clear—
The zoom and whizzing
Of those
Bees.
I froze
Right in my tracks.
"Relax,"
My shoes called up to me;
"All you have to do is push
A bit
And get yourself beyond the
bush."

"I can't," I whispered back.
"The bees will sting me."

"Oh, no, they're easy to outwit.
Just move along with even pace,
And if a bee flies up to you,
Don't wave your hands about
your face
Or otherwise confuse
Him. A bee is nature's
Famed collector
Of a blossom's golden nectar.
He soon will figure out
That you have none,
And he'll go somewhere else to scout."

My two good shoes
Kept telling me
That I could do it.
I took one step
And then another,
But suddenly
A brazen bee
Flew straight at me!
It brushed a breeze
That blew on me.
It jigged and jagged
And zigged and zagged
And hummed its buzz
Right in my ear.
My mouth felt dry
And full of fuzz-
A frightful, dreadful taste!

But I kept my hands down by my waist
And told myself to hold them still.
I moved ahead.
My steps were slow and steady,
And before I even knew it,
I'd left the bush and bees behind.

When I came home from school that day,
My mom was in the kitchen, fixing me
A honey sandwich.
"Hello, there, Davey! How was school?
Is everything okay?
"Well, yes," I said,
"Except my shoes feel tight."
"Are they too small?
You're growing, babe.
You look so tall!"

"I guess you're right,
And, Mom...
Would you please call
Me
Dave."

MAMA'S FIRST PERMANENT WAVE

"A permanent wave is what you need,"
Declared Miz Bertha
As she lifted up a strand
Of Mama's board straight hair.

Miz Bertha was not only
Mama's closest friend,
But in our north Florida country town, in 1925,
She was, as well,
A fount of fashion flair!

And so it was decided,
On that January day.
Along with Mama and my brother Jack,
I climbed into Miz Bertha's black and grey --
Not Ford, not Chevrolet--
But Willys Knight.

True, it was a little old,
Purchased used,
With brakes that didn't hold
Too well.

But off we cruised
To Jacksonville,
A big-time city,
Where one could find a beauty parlor,
Go to movies,
And get stuck behind a streetcar!

Miz Bertha and my Mama
Were absorbed in talk of hair,
And neither of them seemed to care
How close we followed on the trolley.
But for Jack and me it was sheer folly,
And every time the streetcar stopped,
We couldn't swallow due to fright,
Because, in spite
Of all its luxury,
Miz Bertha's spiffy Willys Knight
Had brakes that really were quite iffy.

But we made it somehow to our destination,
And while Mama underwent her transformation,
Jack and I were on our own
To plumb the city's pleasure domes.

We set out on a quest
To find a film about the West
With our heroic superstar, Tom Mix.

A few blocks down the street
There was a double feature.
And so not once, but twice,
We watched our daring hero
Set the West aright. What bliss!

We came out from the theater
when the hour was nearly six.
We knew we'd have to hurry
Since it wouldn't do to miss
The appointed meeting time with
Mama and Miz Bertha.

Now Jacksonville in January,
Especially when the sun has set,
Is subject to a strange state of affairs,
For winds can blow in off the St. John's River
Like an icy polar blast.

My brother Jack and I began to shake and shiver,
And never have there been in all creation
Two boys who ran down city street
On feet so fleet and fast.

We dashed into the parlor,
And we stopped dead in our tracks!
Before us, in a swirl of curls,
A vision of Parisian style and class,
Stood Mama.
And, oh, she looked so pretty!

We drove out of the city
In Miz Bertha's Willys Knight,
And we arrived at our front door
Well pleased with what had been achieved.

Our journey had been safely made
In spite of faulty brakes.
We'd watched our clean-cut cowboy save the day.
But best of all,
Our Mama's board straight hair
Was banished from her life forever more.

PESKY AND THE PEPPERS

It was my mother's plan to arm
Her children with a pleasing appellation,
With a simple designation,
And thus discourage the temptation
To diminish with diminutives
Our dignity and charm.

Much to her alarm, however,
Her intentions were deflected
By her spouse, who readily selected
Names that suitably reflected
The unique and salient features
Of the offspring he had sired.

And so, instead of Grace,
My father was inspired
To call me Pesky.
It's not that I was aggravating...
Oh, no! But I was amazingly creative
And could think of the most clever things to do.

Of course my father had a nickname
For my sister Norma, too.
Not just because she was so blonde and fair,
The very picture of a baby polar bear,
Did he dub my sister "Cub."
But also since she never pondered,
She just pounced feet first into the play of life.

Please note that pouncing unannounced
Upon her older siblings
Seemed to be, for her, a source of utter joy,
For if the truth be told, as indeed it must,
In any physical encounter with our little sister,
We older ones were left behind just rolling in the dust

Once, in contented contemplation
Of the beauty of our garden,
I found myself drawn by a force,
Mysterious and irresistible,
Toward a certain plant: one filled with
Shiny, spicy peppers.
And at that fateful moment
Who should suddenly appear right by my side,
As if by magic?
Why, it was none other than my little sister!

"Mmm, mmm," I said, pointing to the peppers,
"They look so good!
I could eat one, and then you could."
I picked a tiny green one, quite unripe,
And from the end I took a bitsy bite.
"Yum-yum," I said, "it's your turn now!"

And just as I expected,
My sister plucked a pepper
That was fire engine red.
She opened wide her mouth, and chomp!
The shrieks and stomps that followed
Were but a natural expression
Of a lesson great in value;
Appearances, my sister learned,
Can be a dire deception.

But there was yet more knowledge
To be garnered on that day.
When I went in the house, you see,
My sister ran in after me
And lost no time in stuffing something in my mouth.
I bit on it instinctively, and gasped,
And sputtered, and at last spit out
A blazing, bright red pepper.

But as luck would have it, this vindictive act
Was witnessed by our mother, who lacked
All knowledge of the earlier event.
And so it was my sister's fate
To face the dreaded dressing down
Used by our mother when we stood in need
Of understanding that we erred in word or deed.
My sister went to bed that night
A bit more worldly wise.
For those who think that might makes right
Are in for a surprise!

CAMPING IN THE SMOKIES

No sooner had ten-year-old Ray joined the Boy Scouts than adventure was under way. Together with the scoutmaster, the assistant, and the other scouts, he set out from Florida for the troop's annual camping trip in the Smoky Mountains. The day was drawing to an end when they arrived at their camping site, with its spacious clearing among the trees and a mountain stream nearby.

After setting up their pup tents among the trees, the boys built a fire in the middle of the clearing. It was supper time, and they were hungry--so hungry that not even burning the beans, the hot dogs, and the marshmallows prevented their savoring every bite!

When they had finished eating, it was Ray's turn, as the new member, to undergo the troop's traditional initiation ceremony. The rest of the boys gathered up everything they could find that was sticky and gooey—such as jelly and honey and mushy marshmallows. They enthusiastically smeared them all over Ray's face, arms, and clothes. The ritual was supposed to end with Ray's washing off in the mountain stream, but like all mountain streams, it was icy cold. "There's no way I'm getting in that water," Ray said. "I'll just take these napkins and clean myself off." He wiped and swiped a bit and then declared, "Good enough."

Now, what would a camping trip be without a ghost story? The boys gathered around the camp fire, for their scout master always had a good one.

"Boys," he said,
"The Smokey Mountains have their lore
From long before
The Europeans came across the seas.
These mountains were the home of Cherokees.
Perhaps they walked among these very trees
That stand around us now.

For sure they told this story...

One early morning, in the spring,
A brave, young Cherokee
Took up his arrows and his bow
And told his people he would go
Far up into the mountains
In search of wild game.

The hours passed, and when the sun was low
He came into a forest filled
With smoke-like mist.
It seemed to him that he'd been kissed

By some kind woodland sprite,
For right before him stood his prey—
A bear, as black as night.

'You do not want to kill me,' said the bear.
'For if you come with me,
To you the gift I'll give
Is knowing how we black ones live.'

The young man wasn't one to turn
His back upon adventure.
The bear walked on, and by its side,
The Cherokee, with free and eager stride.

At last the two came to a cave,
And there, for many months,

The Cherokee lived with his guide.
When winter came, he realized
That he was covered now with thick, dark hair
Just like the black fur of the bear.
He'd grown accustomed to the fare
Of berries, fruits, and nuts.
He acted like a bear,
Though still he walked upright.

One early morning, in the spring,
They heard the sounds of hunters.
'The hunters are your people,' said the bear.
'And their dogs will find my lair.
The men will kill me with their arrows
And they'll cut me up for meat.
But you they'll not mistreat.
They'll want to take you back with them,
And surely you will go.
But you must do exactly as I say,
For you are now a bear man.

'For seven days you must remain alone.
You cannot see a soul
Or eat or drink at all.
When seven days have passed,
You'll be a man again,
And you can live among your kin.'

'Before you leave with them,
Make certain that you cover up my blood,
And as your people take you home,
Look back, and you will see
A mystery.'

It happened as the bear foretold.

The hunters killed the black one
And cut it into pieces, for its meat.
They recognized the hairy man who stood upright.
They urged him to come back with them
And try to change his wild bear ways.

While all the rest were packing up the meat,
The bear man covered up the black one's blood.
Then, as the party left and he looked back,
He saw a bear rise up and walk into the cave.

The hunters brought the bear man home,
And he went off to be alone
And fast for seven settings of the sun.
But every day his parents called for him
And begged him to come out.

Three days went by, and on the fourth,
When he no longer could withstand their pleas,
He came out from among the trees.
His body still was covered with thick hair.
He walked upright, but like a bear
On its hind legs.

His parents didn't care;
It didn't matter how he looked or how he walked.
'Come be with us,' they cried,
And he complied.

But he was not a man and could not live as one.
Before three days had passed,
The black one came to claim him,
And the bear man breathed his last."

The scoutmaster now concluded his story. "To this very day, he said, "one can see up on these mountains the ghosts of two black bears, side by side. One walks on all fours, and the other walks upright."

The boys crowded in together a little closer and looked all around. Whew--no bears in sight!

"Tell us another story," they begged. But it was late and time for bed.

Ray crawled into his sleeping bag, too tired to change into pajamas. Soon everyone was sound asleep. During the night, however, Ray woke up; his head was bobbling along on the ground, *buh-dup, buh-dup, buh-dup.* He lifted his head and saw in front of him a large, black bear. Ray's sleeping bag, the part down by his feet, was in the bear's mouth, along with all those teeth.

Ray set a record for speed when he bolted from his bag and raced back to the scoutmaster's tent. "A bear...a bear... a big black bear...," he stammered. "It dragged me out of my tent!"

"What's that?" asked the scoutmaster. "A bear dragged you out of your tent? Oh, that's a good one, son. I haven't heard that one before!"

Ray insisted that it had really happened, and reluctantly the scoutmaster and the assistant decided to check things out. In the clearing they found his sleeping bag, which was thoroughly gnawed and clawed.

At last they understood that Ray had told the truth.
Well, not quite all of it.

The detail that Ray didn't share
Was that he saw two bears that night—
The one that had his sleeping bag
Was walking on all fours.
The second bear walked by its side, upright!

THE TALE OF THE BOYISH BOB

It was heaven on earth
At my grandparents' farm,
Near the north Florida town of McAlpin.

There was never a dearth
Of amusements in store,
With the horses and cows,
Juicy melon and cane,
And family members galore.

My aunts Verna and Hazel were older than I,
But just barely,
So that made us all
About ten years of age
That fair summer when
Boyish bobs were the rage,

That fair summer when my uncle Willard, the barber,
Came back to the farm for a visit.
He lined us girls up for a haircut.

Our new look was quite ... modern.
For the rest of the day,
We did nothing but strut
Through the house
And admire our new bobs,
Our new boyish
And very short bobs.

Just a few brief days later
When I had to leave,
All we kids clambered into the back
Of my grandparents' old, flat-bed truck,
And with Grandpa we drove to Aunt Lou's.
Louisiana was one of my grandfather's sisters.
She lived in the city of Jacksonville,
Close to the station
Where I would embark
On my train trip to Santos and home.

We got up bright and early
The following day
And sat down at the table.
The blessing was asked,
But before we could pass
The hot grits and the ham
And the blackberry jam,
Our newly wed aunt said these words
To her spouse:
"I can't possibly eat any breakfast,

Dear George, if you don't come and give me a kiss."

We three girls--Verna, Hazel and I--
Found this statement
To be utterly weird!
Our eyes opened wide
As we peered at each other.
We wiggled and giggled
And wiggled some more.

But then Granpa said, "Young-uns!"
And we knew that we'd best sit up straight and behave.

After breakfast was over, we went to the station.
I boarded the train and was sent off with waves.
When we rolled into Santos, I gathered my baggage,
Smoothed down my new bob,
And majestically stepped from the car,
Where my mother and sisters were waiting to greet me.

Their reaction was far from what I had expected.
There was no applause,
No prolonged oohs and aahs,
And no gasps of appreciative raves.
"What in the world have you done to your hair?"
Asked my mother in stunned disbelief,
While my sisters just stared.

But when she divined that the
Wizard of scissors
Behind the affair
Was none other than her brother Willard,
My mother declared with an air of relief,
"Well, everyone knows that hair always grows."

And that's how it was,
As the twenties roared on,
That I fully forsook
My untoward, boyish bob look.

THE RHODE ISLAND RED ROOSTER

'Twas with great expectation
That Papa brought home
The twenty-odd Rhode Island Reds.
He had thought when he bought them—
The hens and one rooster—
That the money we made
From the eggs that were laid
Would be a big boost to his pay.

But the sad dissipation of anticipation
Was not long in coming.
"No wonder you got such a deal,"
Mama told him.
"Just look at those hens—why, they're on their last legs!
You can count on a pitiful number of eggs."

For Big Red, the Rhode Island Red rooster,
However, the hens in his harem had not lost appeal.
While it may have been so
That indeed they were no young spring chickens,
Every note that he crowed only served to proclaim
His undying desire to defend them.

Although any intruder upon his domain
Faced a painful encounter with avian ardor,
In Big Red's role as guard
Of the fenced-in back yard,
What stood out was his strange predilection
For choosing as victims the feminine sex.
We were never quite sure what made women
So tempting a target.
Perhaps their bare legs
Were a beacon too bright to ignore.

Big Red staged his attacks from the side,
With great stealth,
And unflagging, unsagging in purpose and pride,
He would fly at the leg of his prey
With great flapping of wings
And a banshee-like cry,
The sharp spurs on his claws at the draw.

There were numerous reasons to open the gate
And venture inside Big Red's fort.
One, of course, was to gather the eggs that were laid
Now and then by the hens.
And to get to the outhouse there was but one route.
It led straight through the red rooster's court.
In addition, the heavy, black cauldron for boiling our clothes
Never strayed from its post in the yard

That Big Red had appointed himself to defend.

Now, outside the battle zone, right by the gate
Was a long, wooden axe handle.
It offered to Big Red's opponents
A fair, fighting chance
To counter the outcome of his devilish dance,
And as time drifted by,
Big Red learned from experience
That messing with Mama was not a wise move.

But nonetheless eager to prove his great prowess,
He kept Wilma, the wash woman, high on his list.
It took both her hands when she tended the cauldron,
And that left her powerless then to resist
Big Red's method of shifty attack.

The rooster would trumpet,
And Wilma would wail;
You'd think it was Judgment Day
Coming for real!

Finally, Wilma grew tired of it all,
And she hatched up a plan of her own.
She asked for permission to take Big Red home.
"I'll break him of that nasty habit," she said.
I remember my mama's faint little smile
As she gave her assent.

As the days became weeks, I began wondering why
Wilma didn't bring old Big Red back.
When I voiced my concern,
That faint smile played across Mama's face.
"Oh, my goodness," she said, "don't you stew about that!
That ornery rooster was one tough old bird,
And in taking him on, Wilma no doubt bit off
More than she found she could chew!"

The red rooster's departure brought in a new age,
And tranquility reigned in the unguarded yard.
Although Wilma had sworn to reform him,
That Rhode Island Red sure proved stubborn in crime,
For we plain didn't see the old bird any more.
I guess Wilma chewed for a mighty long time!

ABOUT THE AUTHOR

Joyce's storytelling career began 25 years ago when she shared a favorite Russian folk tale with her son's third grade class. Since then she has told her stories in a number of venues besides American (and Costa Rican) schools and libraries: festivals, concerts, story slams, churches, parks, coffee houses, retirement homes, and, once, with passengers in a car that had pulled over to wait for an Arizona dust storm to run its course. The kinds of stories she tells mirror the same wide-ranging variety, from personal tales that are based on her own experience to folk tales that capture the wisdom of generations of entire peoples.

Her book, *The Rhyme and Rhythm of Childhood*, features stories inspired by childhood memories that family and friends have shared with her. Set mostly in North Florida, these stories reflect and honor the culture into which she was born. Formal studies in Romance and Slavic languages and literatures, however, as well as extended periods of living abroad, have ensured her deep appreciation for traditions different from her own, wherever they are encountered.

Joyce holds a Ph.D. in Slavic languages and literatures and is a retired college educator in the fields of her formal academic training as well as in the art of storytelling.

A storyteller at the White Tank Mountain Regional Park in the Phoenix area, she currently writes and shares stories about the plants and animals of the Sonoran Desert.

21328231R00027

Made in the USA
Charleston, SC
14 August 2013